Another Love, Another Life

Graeme Hetherington
Another Love, Another Life

Acknowledgements

Acknowledgement is due to the following,
where these poems first appeared:
*The Age, The Adelaide Review, Antipodes, The Australian,
The Australian Book Review, The Canberra Times,* Ginninderra Press,
*Imago, Island, LiNQ, The Mozzie, Poetry Australia, Poetry Matters,
Quadrant, Studio, Valley Micropress, Westerly.*

Another Love, Another Life
ISBN 978 1 76041 970 7
Copyright © Graeme Hetherington 2020
Cover image: Gay Hawkes, *Couple*, made in Yerevan, Armenia, 2013

First published 2020 by
GINNINDERRA PRESS
PO Box 3461 Port Adelaide 5015
www.ginninderrapress.com.au

Contents

1

Runaways	11
Schools of Thought	13
Curios 1999 and Everything Must Go 2003	15
Phobias	17
What's in a Name?	19
Artemis and Actaeon	20
Artemis and Actaeon (2)	22
Daedalus	24
Dead Twin	25

2

To the Island	29
Frontier Foundation – 1994	30
Young Couple in Developing Landscape	31
A Tasmanian–English Tale	33

3

The Sexual Bonding of Gilgamesh and Enkidu	37
Bill and Gwen	39
But for Poetry Chaos and Madness	40
Encounter	41

4

The Return of Eve	47
For Anton Holzner	49
Blackman's Bay Garden	51
For Helen as Soulmate	54
Intimations of Disaster	59
Restless	63

5

Australians at War in Europe	67
Reprieves in England, Italy, Spain and Crete	69
Runaways (2)	73
Release	75

6

An Expatriate's Lament	79

7

Dashed Prospects in Crete	89
Theseus	90
For Vetta	92
Femme Fatale	97

8

Rendezvous in Nice	103
A Need to Explain	105
Belvedere Gardens, Vienna	106
For my Czech Stepdaughter	107
In Memory of Dr Ivana Gajdošová 1944–2013	110

9

A Thank You to a Polish Musician	115
Breaking the Ice	117
For Robyn Mathison	118
Aesthetically Speaking	119
Adam Tempted to Give Eve Flowers	121
St Helen's Road	122

'Love comes disguised as a summer without flaws,
but the golden light hides the intricate spider's web'
Andrew M. Bell

1

Runaways

(But for rumours of arson –)

A timber mill owner burnt out,
Not once but twice, grandfather moved
Under a cloud of rumour from

New Zealand to Tasmania. Forced
To find work in the island's West
Coast mining town of Rosebery,

His credentials qualified him,
Since bad weather and secrecy
About the past were part of life,

Not even Roaring Forties' rain
Able to get rid of 'the stain',
The alcoholic old lags washed

In from the Hell's Gates' hinterland.
But for his wowser-wife and five
Teenage daughters to end up there,

A natural as well as man-
Made wilderness cutting them off
From a politer world they'd known

Was a traumatising comedown.
Always in black, hat with veil raised
Only to scold and scare, my fierce

Nay-saying gran seemed mostly to
Use it as dark glasses are now,
Though not so much to combat sun-

Light as the glaring ugliness,
Hide deep shame at her fate, her grim
Judgemental moral outrage from

A people more carefree, and which
Became my mother's need to draw
The curtains close to keep the Arch

Fiend from our home, mine to drink with
The enemy as I searched for
A breath of liberating air.

Schools of Thought

Locked out of classrooms we ate our
Cribs brought from home in 'shelter sheds',
Though they were open to the West

Coast's almost daily wind and rain.
One for each sex and built apart
At opposite ends of the yard,

The head made lightning raids but failed
To keep us separate. I learnt
Not to expect too much, since far

From ideal, my 'better half's' talk
Demeaned no less than that of boys,
Pasties tasting as a fart smells,

Menstrual rags of rotten fish.
Then sent to a male boarding school
At thirteen I was able to

Indulge my horror of the flesh,
Become a Dante mooning for,
No real Beatrice glimpsed as soulmate,

But a mentally perilous,
Totally insubstantial dream,
A hope that an as yet unknown

Form of perfection would appear,
Recognised as such when it did.
Disastrously, it never has,

My marriages, affairs, wrecked by
The shadow of pure abstract thought
That at most she was second best.

Curios 1999 and *Everything Must Go 2003*

(After two paintings by David Keeling)

If it had been my lot to live,
As my unhappy mother did,
Beneath a mountain blocking out
Escape into a view of sea

Or sky, upon a foothill cleared
And levelled dead-flat to create
A government housing estate,
I would have done the same, gone mad,

Drawn blinds and curtains, opted for
'The Great Indoors' among a mix
Of in-all-shades of cardboard-brown,
Affordably cheap thinnish sticks

Of furniture. For company I
Too might in bitterness have bought
Shiny black bulbous skull shapes, bowls
Of venom standing on about-

To-scurry spider legs, and on
Poised, elegantly supple, curved
Octopus tentacles. They brought
Back memories of the head, she said,

Of spastic cousin Ian shaved
For surgery, and Uncle Neil's
Dark from a booze-induced burst vein.
And I too, lonely and withdrawn,

Grown just as desperate and inclined
To perversity, would have named
And talked to them for years on end,
But I had better luck, a kind

Of clearance of the mind, and threw
Life in the suburbs on the tip,
Both her insane interior
And world beyond the lounge peeped at:

Garage and jumble sales, those draw-
Card weekend technicolour shows
Of gimcrack bits and pieces, junk
No sooner acquired than piled up

On corpse-grey concrete pavements for
Ten dollars, dear at half the price,
And which she always saw as too
Beneath her ever to attend,

And finally just couldn't for
The angst that shook her at the thought,
A panic attack killing as
She clung at ninety to an arm-

Less curio for comfort in
Her hour of need, the favourite of
The collection, which though poisonous
She still preferred to other folk.

Phobias

(Renison Bell, West Coast, Tasmania)

1

My father and my brother drawn
Together sharing skills of which
I was devoid, my mother cold,
Unbridgeably remote and lost

In her defeat, I had no one
To love until my sister came.
Then to exuberant release
Of joy it was snapped 'No!' and 'Don't!'

From a horror of incest said
To occur in derelicts' shacks
And lean-tos in our mining town
That drove me further from the fold.

2

At first light, over and again,
Shrill and clear, for many days now,
A bird cries 'Innocent!' as though
It would acquit me, self-arraigned

And judged guilty since childhood, when
Parents had caused me to lie face
To the wall in the bedroom shared
With my sister, afraid to see

Her there, let alone go to sleep,
In case, to cut the knot of my
Growing confusion about her,
Guard down, I'd walk across and kill.

3

I used to keep myself awake,
Watch moonlight on my sister's hair
Turn bloody and run down her face
Of pale angelic purity
My mother wouldn't let me touch,

Or if my night-long vigil failed
I'd wake from dreams in which she died
And cross the bedroom floor to see
If I had killed her in my sleep,
Relieved if I could hear her breathe.

What's in a Name?
(Courting poem for G)

Disturbed, I cast you, just because
You were called 'Archer', in the role
Of huntress-goddess Artemis,

Avenger of young innocents,
Such as my sister was, whom I'd
Harmed with my love. And then you wed

And became 'Unicombe' that trans-
Lates loosely from Old English as
'A valley sweet as honeycomb'.

It augurs well for us should you
Decide to keep it on now we've
Been freed by deaths to meet and feel

As though fifty plus years apart
Were no longer than arrows take
From Cupid's bow to reach the heart,

My madness in seeing you as
Nemesis for a childhood sin
Caused and cured by the power of names.

Artemis and Actaeon

1

Divinely beautiful, bow-drawn,
Praxitilean Artemis,
Avenging goddess of the young
And innocent, you ambushed me

The evening I saw, decades on
From boyhood's crime of sister love,
You smiling darkly like her in
My Greek host's maiden-daughter's eyes.

2

She was eighteen to my three score
When I tried at dinner one night,
By studying the other guests,
My cutlery, then the new moon

To avoid her eye, and you snapped
What I thought was my iron control,
Drowning me, way out of my depth
In her steadfast lunar-lit gaze.

3

Unerringly, you struck again,
When she in front of parents, who
Knew little English, told me I
Was not a father-figure, but
A man to her. Such bold deceit

Was warning that she served your end
To bring me low, as was her face,
As seemingly indifferent to
The consequences of love as
Your statue's pitiless regard.

4

And then she disappeared to take
Up dentistry in Athens while
I stayed and pulled love's teeth in tense

Hair-trigger Crete, meeting again
Months later in her father's yard,
Feelings for each other intact.

Lone foreigner among quick-eyed
Gossiping relatives, I sensed
The interest of starved chained watchdogs

In bare white bones thrown out of reach
Shift to my bald but skin-browned head,
Aching fit to split wide from angst,

Imagined them freed, closing in,
Growls louder as I fled on foot,
Actaeon's antlers on my brow

Promising even richer food,
The crescent moon bending to loose
The punishment feared all my life.

Artemis and Actaeon (2)

(For my eye specialist)

1

So like my sister glimpsed in Greek
Nude statuary as Artemis,
Avenging goddess of those harmed

When young and innocent, as she
Was by my childhood love, you twang
Her bowstring, lasering my eye

With arrows, tuning me to song:
Released from marble she's less cruel
Alive as you, just hard to win

Now on account of youth and age,
Not made impossible as work
Of art, nor outlawed as incest.

Therefore be warned, that you, instead
Of caring for my retina
Should shoot me dead with shafts of light,

Since my good orb, trained on you, lost,
Absorbed completely in your task,
Exposed as one is without clothes,

Intensely showers you with lust's barbs
Rather than worships and adores
Platonically as an old man.

2

Again, suddenly, there you were,
Quite unaware of me, and this
Time in a portside restaurant,

So that my feeling like a stunned
Old mullet was appropriate.
Then later that same evening, by

Coincidence I sat one row
Diagonally behind you at
A concert as Beethoven, Bach

And Mozart all pined for love lost,
Observing you, oblivious
And vulnerable, afraid you'd turn

And slay me with a look, as did
The goddess with real arrows once
Actaeon peeping as she bathed.

Daedalus

The labyrinth I built foretold
The dark confusion of my life,
So riddled with intrigue and crime
Inspired by jealousy to keep

Craft secrets and my image as
Supreme inventor safe, that it's
A wonder I'm not mad. I killed
My nephew Talos for his skill,

For being first to conceive of
The compass, saw and potter's wheel.
Unless what drove me to it was
His incest with his mother, my

Sister I'd failed to lure to bed
With strategies more subtle than
Poor Pasiphaë spread in a cow.
Now Icarus, my son, is dead,

His wing feathers not sewn on
Like mine, but stuck in place with wax,
Because I knew he'd try to fly
Much higher than I'd ever dare,

Which leaves me on my own to age
With growing shame and guilt, to find
A way out from my caved-in self,
The minotaur about to pounce.

Dead Twin

(For Gianna Kriezotou)

Eyes locking in recognition,
We became lovers overnight,
And after we had soothed the beast
Of longing for 'the other', she,

As we lay back to back, explained
The scarred lump on her tailbone: joined
To a sister, surgically freed
She alone survived. And when I

Reciprocated with my loss
Of mine from fits of jealous rage
I learnt it didn't correspond,
That her guilt was much more profound,

Beyond her mental powers to cope
Except through an obsession with
The horoscopes for Gemini,
Whom she, a Greek, preferred to call

The *dioskouroi*, though in fact
They were Capricorns. Her farewell,
In red lipstick upon the bed-
Room's dusty and cracked mirror was

Signed 'Castor and Pollux'. I found
Her with an old flame butting out
On her flesh, turning it to trays
Full of ash. Scornfully she said,

Of my shock, dismay and concern,
'You don't understand,' to go
Away and write her epitaph,
And to console myself I did:

Gathering the scattered residue,
The fine grey dust of both, Zeus formed
Two stars from it, decreeing they
Should shine forever as the Twins.

2

To the Island

(After a painting by David Keeling)

Black-framed, the scene's a mourning card,
Since I could be the man who rows
The woman to a rock shaped as

Tasmania upside down. My wife,
I wed too quickly to know her
Untransplantable English side,

She stands to rock the boat and take
Advantage of ambivalence,
My deep-rooted conflict about

Whether this outcrop of forlorn
Alcatraz-like rock in the south,
My native isle, is truly home,

Her mind made up she'll drown before
Setting foot there, yet staying till
After seven years broken by

Clinics, ECT, me, I took
Her and our girls back, leaving them
In London where we'd met, for what

Then seemed would be our mutual good,
Only to learn, as it turned out,
I'd circumscribed my life with grief.

Frontier Foundation – 1994

(After a painting by David Keeling)

Again the woman in one of
Your paintings could be my first wife,
The archetypal whingeing Pom

Of doubtful pioneering stock
As gormlessly, caved-in she sits
Slumped and supported by an arm

On a building's foundation bricks
In the nearly empty countryside
Of Van Diemen's Land, the Devil's isle,

Her new home. Quite unable to
Make a go of it, depression has
Deepened from life among the bones

Of murdered blacks beneath her feet,
And strengthening her attitude
Of 'what is left to make me try?'

Brought on psychotic episodes,
Hallucinations to judge from
Her startled look, the other hand

Raised in terror from the surprise:
Five thin dark lines encroaching on
The foreground like prongs of a pitch-

Fork she alone sees the rest of,
And who wields it, moving towards
Her from beyond the picture's frame.

Young Couple in Developing Landscape
(After a painting by David Keeling)

Your portrait of a youthful pair
Posed toffee-nosed, smug among signs
Of rurally provincial art
And crudely cruel history that's warped
The Tasmanian descendants of

The felons of Van Diemen's Land
Could easily be seen as one
Of Graeme and Susan Hetherington
Blown in as Lord and Lady Muck
To scornfully ignore such things

As just colonial bad taste.
The first a native white escaped
To culturally richer Greece
In an attempt to change his roots,
The second measuring all by her

Superior Pom origins,
They're blind to Glover-eucalypts
Snaking out to asphyxiate
Them for their studied arrogance,
To bones of blacks lying around,

Waiting to resurrect and trip
Them into a convict-dug pit
That in conceit they overlook
Although close to the edge of it,
Emblem of their crowd-pleasing fall

Into the hell of splitting up,
Bankruptcy, children lost, when she,
Disoriented, dispossessed,
Twice broke down crying out for home,
And he, already there, if but

Contemptuously, cooly took
The opportunity to get
Rid of them, being able to
Wrestle the mess into a poem,
Lives irreversibly destroyed.

A Tasmanian–English Tale

Emotionally volatile, split
In my allegiance, I dumped 'rule
Britannia' wife and daughters back

In 'the old Dart', avenging kin
Transported to Van Diemen's Land
By turning its vile origins

That blighted my home on their head.
Then you, another of her ilk,
Mother Country born and bred, yet

Not imperious, and by luck
Also deserted, left to care
For two young children, came in from

The garden sensuously wet,
As in the T.S. Eliot poem
Celebrating Ash Wednesday.*

Sublime in all your Englishness,
Red roses in your hands not gouts
Of felons' blood but jewels bright,

Transfigured beyond history's reach,
Time standing still as my held breath,
It seemed to make good loss, restore

My convict-and-the-lady dream,
Now that I'd evened up the score
And my proud heart had grown contrite.

---

* The first day of Lent; so called from the custom introduced by Pope Gregory the Great of sprinkling ashes on the heads of penitents on that day.

3

The Sexual Bonding of Gilgamesh and Enkidu

(For James McAuley)

1

My right to be the first with brides
Depends not just on being two-
Thirds god and king, but on how well

I read signs in red roses, blood-
Flushed symbols of male sexual pride.
Although no gardener, I alone

Attend their needs, admire, delouse,
Prune, water, wear, let none within
A bull's roar to ensure that I

Monopolise such power. They've bloomed
Less fully lately, and on dry
Thin brittle stems new thorny growth

Surrounds, choking to signify
The bridegrooms' rising. While this bud
In haughty isolation curled

Suggests a rival, a young man
Who's to be either nipped and thrown
Upon the compost heap, or dubbed

Soulmate and used to help out with
My exercising of *droit de
Seigneur* among more maidens than

I've appetite for now I'm doomed,
Cankered with cancer like the flowers.
Literally covering for me, he,

Rewarded with joy, then at least
Can be called on to bear his fair
Share of the husbands' mounting wrath.

2

Presenting me with a red rose
She then joined me in bed, her flow
Of auburn hair a tent of fire
Enfolding us as we embraced,
Brightening and flaring, as she said
'I come as priestess, courtesan,
From Gilgamesh who's known me,
Empowered thus to give his gift
Of love. Received, it will free you
Trapped in the wilderness of need.'
And afterwards I woke to sun
That seemed at first to be his face,
This poem my flower in return,
Forty years on since it was sown.

Bill and Gwen

In Swiftian mood, insisting that
The human race would never learn,
Was hopeless, doomed, Bill Harwood, pure
Logician and philosopher,
As well as spouse of poet Gwen,

Proposed a universal ban
On sex to end our sorry ways
And brought our threesome's talk on how
The world was going to a halt
Of the socially awkward kind.

Then magically, as tension grew,
As though specifically she knew
This impasse would arise, she whipped
A book up from her lap and showed,
Spread open at the very page,

A photo of a rationalist
And his divinely inspired wife,
Of Abelard and Heloise,
Their mediaeval counterparts
As sculpted on a column in

The Conciergerie, Paris,
His castrated parts cupped by her
Protectively as in a nest,
Their stooped backs turned forever on
Each other in a bed of stone.

But for Poetry Chaos and Madness

Gwen Harwood, highly strung and prone
To histrionics claimed that once
While waiting in a fish and chip

Shop to be served she saw a page
Of newspaper that had a poem
Of hers on it being wrapped round

A bit of flake, and felt chewed up,
Then swallowed in a gulp, as if
Watching *Jaws* all over again.

Lying in her teeth, I admit
To thinking as she told this tale,
Until big-eyed and tense in what

Seemed a sincere onslaught of fear
She startled, changing my mind with
'Black covering the screen-door buzzed

Like Christ Crucified's face with flies',
And by conceiving these lines, no
Matter how dark the images,

Swam for dear life away from worse,
Structuring panic with form found
Before its dismantling rush drowned.

Encounter

1

A loving daughter, mother, wife,
Safe, run-of-the-mill, middle- class
Bourgeois teacher in private schools,

Poet and critic on the side
In defence of the status quo,
Hatred and jealousy of those

With an original talent
That take them well beyond the pale
Drove her to embrace the role of

Inquisitor of heretics.
Without trying to find out why
I'd come to detest family life,

She, with politically correct,
Socially sanctioned sentiments
Condemned my poems to be burnt on

A bonfire in the public square,
For matricide and patricide,
Fratricide and sororicide,

And hoped my victims met me in
The afterlife to inflict all
The torment in revenge she said

I'd claimed as 'fantasist' to have
Borne as a boy from my folk who
Found me too sensitive for them.

2

Hair cropped, tense-faced, giraffish, gaunt,
With raw-boned washerwoman's hands,
A feminist descended from

Nathaniel Hawthorne's puritans,
Her criticisms scrubbed my soul
She'd called misogynistic too,

Again without supportive facts,
Except 'regardless of sex he
Kills family off across the board'.

I dwelt on her review until
She was a blackbird patiently
Perched on a branch as dark and bare

As winter can accomplish, seen
On walks, in dreams, and in the bath-
Room mirror each day as I shaved,

Her beak a maggot-yellow, eyes
Intermittently flashing fire,
Trained on me as intently as

A predatory priestess's
Instruments of torture, as though
A constant ravenous regard

Conceivably might turn me from
An abstract literary meal
Into a real one as a corpse.

3

Having been introduced at last
Mutual attraction grew until
On meeting and on parting we

Would kiss full-lipped, in love the same
Way prey and hunter are. But now
She's read the first two poems of this

Sequence and glimpsed the full extent
Of my malaise, she with due care
Inclines her head, averts her mouth

And cautiously proffers a cheek,
Climaxing in a phone call with
'I don't want to have sex with you.'

4

The Return of Eve

1

Despair is a doll. She chews on her cud
And weeps at the seams. For seven lean years
I ate at her side. She cried for my teeth
To strike solid bone, but I found

Only kapok rotten with damp,
The sadness of cats lying dead in the rain.
Now there is you, slim and supple with joy:
Someone to harvest for seven fat years.

2

(For Carol)

Like black gouts of blood,
Wet clumps of feathers steam
As winter starlings throng
A tree's arthritic limbs
Swollen by the rain.

As deathly still as sentinels,
Also lining limp tuneless wires
Between grey damp fur-coated poles
Grown out of pitch and tar,
They guard the season well.

But your red hair,
Tantalising as a torch parade
Moving in and out of sight
Among chameleon shapes of mist,
Flames suddenly into a crown:

Branches glow, mould dries and flakes,
The slack of strands is taken up
As birds of dark presage take flight,
While feather-light, wing-swift and lit,
Memories of spring usurp the day.

3

(For Helen)

A drummer-boy stands alone in the snow.
Blood flows from his side as he plays without heart
To waterfalls frozen in the chill air,
To his shadow that leads from him like a road.

He can see skiing towards him a girl
With summer-blue eyes that sing a white song
As she enters his side and the waterfalls flow:
It is time for him now to come in from the cold.

For Anton Holzner

1

(Paris to Menelaus)

Your marriage lay in ruins from the start.
God-given joy is usually on loan,
And at nineteen how could she really know
What Aphrodite would find out in her?

Like all of us, you based your trust
In present time and built a castle in the air.
It is my luck to have her now and please
One goddess out of three. But what of next?

My future could be as your present is
Since mortals change as quickly as their gods.
Achilles' rage now breaks on Troy, and Helen dreams
Each night of towers swept under by the wine-dark sea.

2

(Paris to Hector)

'A stallion always after mares,
A pretty boy who shirks the war,'
You sneered at me before the troops
To cure me of my lover's ways,

But there will come a day, an hour,
A moment when you'll be unmanned,
Achilles treading on your heels.
Instead of one swift arrow shot

To fell the killer in mid-stride,
I'll string my bow in Helen's bed
Until he's shamed you with his hands,
Your titbits given to the dogs.

Blackman's Bay Garden

1

You've painted out the house within
A week of it becoming ours.
Married before, like you, but much
The older, I've nursed fears that you'll
Run wild as blackberries down the back,

While on our weathered door, sunlight
Netted by shadows from tree leaves
Trembles, about to flee, as does
My trust when you say such things as
'Another love, another life!'

2

My childhood oak, as large as life,
Was there for a split second in
Place of the willow that now hangs

Over our home. I hid up high,
A hunted, outcast 'ciss', daydreamed
In compensating scorn myself

Into a prince, but one who must
Have sensed the fantasy was no
More than half true until he'd joined

His princess, also hurt, to live
In melancholy exile from
The world beneath a weeping tree.

3

The willow spoke in golden tones,
Through leaves that flowed like waterfalls,
Through coin that never-ending ran,

Each piece minted by the sun.
Today they hacked its branches off
To give someone the telephone.

With saws, blunt instruments and ropes,
It takes four hours to kill the tree,
Load limbs and torso on the truck,

Fronds dragging on the road like hair.
The driver and his mate both wave,
A cripple and an amputee.

A tree can never really die,
Its lifeblood doesn't flow away,
And sawdust like a fall of snow

Returns forever to the earth,
As from the stump there rises clear
A column of the purest air.

4

Our briar rose tree richly gave
And now there's summer's aftermath
Papering the burnt-out grass,

While thorn-tipped shoots climb brittle sticks:
I'm old and wish for limbs like yours,
For mine to savage you with love.

5

In summertime's aqua-green light
The long front veranda sets sail
With Adam curled up on his couch,
The sprinkler jets hissing and cool,

Tormenting and bringing him death
As curving they strike at the leaves,
Past Eve stretching out in the sun
Near shadows too lazy to move.

For Helen as Soulmate

1

A photograph of an image
From one of your paintings went round
The luncheon guests quickly enough
Until it was mine to make out,

Obscurely, then coming to life
As washes of blue made to glow
By touches of red for a cap,
A bridle, a tail, a strong arm

Attaching to me as I heard
'Thank you for looking to see it,'
Myself astride, sweeping you up
To gallop us out of the room.

2

Our bedroom window's draped in heavy blue,
Lovemaking spends us and we get up late.
You've drawn 'Today' to live in there with us:

A curtain swept back from a bed,
The grey dead flesh risen into white
And sunlight tearing at the clouds.

3

The Bach-crisp pencil lines against
Soft greys and blues on ringing white
Have rendered themes of love and death

As timelessly as time itself.
Your hand's a lifeline to simple human truth,
To hearts where passion dying flares white-hot.

4

Your mother's coronary shocked new
Love's millpond like a stone thrown in.
To try and spread the circles till
They fade, if not quite disappear,

We need to say she smoked, was old
And overweight, to rationalise,
Subdue fears that we were to blame,
Since even though she blessed us when

You left a fellow-painter more
Mad-keen on his work than on you,
For me obsessed with poems, she may
Have had her doubts as well, a heart-

Felt undertow that dragged her down,
Insidiously whispering 'She's
Survived her folly for Art once,
This time, out of her depth, she'll drown.'

5

You sit propped up in bed and paint
The black umbrellas in the street
As coloured petals on a stream.
Another one of many days

To be endured with images,
The pageant of the rush hour fades
And leaves you with a sea of death
That drowns the scattered flowers you'd saved.

6

As flesh wastes on the human frame
And skeletons disintegrate,
Snow melts and ribs a mountain range,
Allows the darkness to emerge

Until it overtakes the bones.
With charcoal in your frozen hand
You started drawing it at dawn
Despite the sharp pain in your side.

7

I'm scared your chronic lung disease
Will leave you ugly in old age,
That I will fail to love you then
And sentimentalise my song

To celebrate you for the world
As golden-limbed and beautiful
As you were on the day we met,
As Bonnard painted his sick wife

When she was over sixty-five,
Like Venus glowing from the bath
And bending as the goddess would
To dry the insides of her thighs.

8

The scene as you lay ill in bed
Reminded me of Munch's *Sick Child*,
Except that I replaced the dark
Stooped mother-figure sitting near,
And as his fellow-artist watched

Your face, similarly stark white
And vulnerable in profile on
A matching pillow looking cold,
Hard as a slab of marble in
A butcher's shop displaying meat.

Your hair also could have been hers,
A mess of red strands salt from sweat
Was stiffening, and which I thought
Might rise up like a nest of snakes,
Electrify the fetid air

And strike you mad. His thinking too,
As predator, if only half
Of what's come down about his life
Is true. As well though, he and I,
By noting that the eye expressed

A dreamily detached, quiet joy,
The certain knowledge that death would
Release the soul to something else,
Declared you both beyond all our
Attempts to pin with paint and words.

9

(Orpheus)

O Eurydice, you've become
A shadow lying in my arms,
A lyre of grief so tightly strung

I have no armament but song
To try and break the heart of Death.
O Eurydice, as we climb,

Blow breath softly through my hair,
Let your mirror be the moon,
Let me know you follow on.

O Eurydice, thin as air,
Give me still the faintest sign,
Let your shadow move near mine.

Intimations of Disaster

1

A brilliant spring day and you ask,
Your pleurisy less painful now,
If we might drive and look out on
A fresh-air world. We're happy with
The play of light on leaves, our sex

Contrived without hurt in the back,
Till watchful as a Brueghel crow
I spot a blush of guilt and tear,
From where lung's sticking still, their names,
Old loves brought here before myself.

You tire, say you forgive, leave me
To shame for having turned your past
Into a small sickroom, probed, pecked,
Black wings around you, in again,
Beak sticky to the eyes with blood.

2

Yellow orange brown and blue,
Paper flowers with black centres wilt
In the X-ray waiting room.
A worn-out protea
Brushed by your fingertips sends up

A tiny puff of dust.
You'll have to wait before you know
If fantasies of wasting flesh
And wreaths grew out of groundless fears
Or intuition based on fact.

3

Your face is sad like roses pressed
Against wet glass, or matchless in its joy
Behind a summer waterfall. Against
A window-pane the rain insists,

Your voice reminding, 'I am yours to know.'
Morning comes, your face wakes cold and hard,
The window cleared to a folded rose:
Beyond compare, waterfalls of joy remain.

4

In my black, white-studded shirt, I
Felt flat as an iron and stiff
As starch, as remote as the night
Sky done up too tightly with stars,
Till you burst it open and showed,

Released from my desperate embrace,
The garden in flower at dawn,
Weaving, for my cleared head, no crown
Of thorns, but one bedewed, as though
Christ-like with sweat I'd fought for love.

5

(After Chekhov's *The Cherry Orchard*)

We loved our first home but we sold
To people now thinning the trees,
The willow with bark like ploughed fields,
The pines reaching higher each year,

Our marriage to heaven and earth.
I think of the sound at play's end,
From a cable snapped meaning doom,
The growth of our new garden slow.

6

(Marion Bay, Tasmania)

Autumn sun leafing our love nest
Unvisited for years, the sea
A hard grey heaving expanse of

Excalibur-embedding rock,
Cats-paws its fragmenting hilt that
Mirrored my lack of desire for

Rejuvenating sex, the day
Cooled with ourselves re-crossing dunes
That became mountains of myth filled

With monsters as we snapped and snarled.
And when we chanced on a lagoon
Where a huge stump floated by like

A funeral barge, a stiff black branch
Sticking up through green sleeving slime,
With mess of twigs and tendrils as

Its hand and fingers seized a strip
Of silver pillaring the sky
And brought night down on our bowed heads.

Restless

1

Far more than pleasing to the eye,
The treasures you've brought to our house.
Plants such as Devil's Ivy, Wandering Jew
And Moses-in-the-Cradle are

The setting for old pottery shards,
Graeco-Roman coins, images
From books on European art,
Migratory birds fashioned from

Metal by an artist-friend, stamps,
Anything with an atmosphere
Of 'abroad', like your camel bell
The antique shop said was a Kurd's,

While a crustacean with a Star
Of David outline whitens in
A nest you found beneath a tree,
Shells sighing, 'Home's across the sea.'

2

Unable to decide, we walked
The beach below our house in search
Of signs to sell or stay, and had
To ward off nesting plovers' dives

Straight at our heads, sank ankle-deep
In sand and then observed a man
Mid-channel climbing carefully up
A swaying rope ladder to mend

A navigation light. He took,
After much trouble, the bulb out,
Its brain that at least flickered still,
And dropped it in the sea, tried all

The new ones after cutting bits
Off veins lying in muddled heaps,
Descended to his boat and left
Us more than ever in the dark.

3

Pain can rinse, illuminate the flesh.
Your face as grave and gentle as a nun's,
I fetch and carry, sit and hold your hand,
Outraged that you should suffer this so young,

Scar tissue on a lung dragging wide awake
A love-child found only a year ago
Like violets in a wilderness of scrub.
You dream of flying, nothing would surprise.

5

Australians at War in Europe

1

To pick and eat, or not, our Fall
Occurred near cloister orange trees,
Where broken hedges guarding them
Beginning to mildew the ground,

And signs in black, not warning red,
We couldn't read to save ourselves,
Were ambiguities that caused
Our row testing perfection's strength,

Till grass, you argued, couldn't be
A 'keep-off' lawn because so long,
Grew Satan-sibilant with 'Stuff
One suppurating in his mouth.'

2

I felt myself mocked by the flowers
Bright yellow and richer than gold,
With love woven into a chain
For my Vandemonian neck.
Unable to stand their loud laugh,

Their sun-happy dance round my head,
I threw the gift back in your face
That closed up as tight as a bud.
Oxalis, you said, was their name,
Though soursob was better for some.

3

The massive wall we walked around
Each day, light-headed from yet one
More sleepless night of fights, had come,
Apparently impregnable,

To stand for all the reasons we
Must stay together despite them.
Then with my fingernail I traced
The granite's blue-grey grain and saw

A butterfly of the same hue
Meandering sun-drunk brush up
Against it and vanish, shoot through
Decisively on my behalf.

4

First walk together since your flu,
I found a frozen pond that shone
As purely as the Virgin's soul,
And you, your feathers ruffled as

I sang in praise of her, the strength
To smash it to smithereens. But,
Her spirit sharply glittering as
It flew, your stone failed to destroy

New love, killing only us, two
Absurdly ill-assorted birds,
And freed my muse to follow her
With scintillating flocks of poems.

Reprieves in England, Italy, Spain and Crete

1

Five-fingered plane leaves blew our way
And pressed in passing on your sick-
Room's windowpane. An envelope,
Postmarked faintly by veins, but with

No contents other than a sky
As empty as our estranged hearts,
It brought us close enough to joke
About God lending you a hand.

2

One morning after heavy rain,
Earthworms were on our bedroom floor.
They raised a segment of themselves,
Each head in search of something more

Than soil washed through and further chilled
On cracked marble. St George without
His armour, horse, lance, castle wall,
I left the warmth our bodies made,

Yours feverish from another cold,
Barehanded threw them far away,
Then drowned my fingers in the sink
Before running them over you.

3

I didn't know the flower's name
And thought of gold tossed at my feet
Before I bent to take it home,

A gift from my long evening walk
For you still ill and left behind
As love that glows among grey stones.

4

Bomb-blast scars upon flagstones,
Soldiers being trained to kill,
Paintings in each run-down church

Of Christ crucified and dead,
Sun like a target on the wall
Of the room where you lie ill.

5

Late winter's isolated flowers
Have lit the stone-strewn ancient fields
As weather-beaten shepherds move
Their golden sheep to safer homes.
Like one of the anemones,

You listen to their tinkling bells
That with the birdsong thrills your soul
As you do mine for good and ill.
I turn to catch your smile and lose
Your pale face in the evening sun.

6

Our dangerous dislike of crowds
Reined tightly in, we gave up on
Attempts to stroll around the walls
As king and queen for scrambling for

Lawn chairs. Enthroned, we bolted, poured
The boiling lead of scorn and made
Joke fodder of the hordes, with 'Up
You' signs explained away to those

Provoked enough to ask, as tea
For two or double gin requests
To waiters on the run. Sides split,
Eyes filled with tears, collapsing at

A finger raised to test if our
Hysteria had passed, we then,
For physical and mental ease,
Scraped back, dug grass up with hind legs,

Till court dwarves in the livery of
The Borgia or Medici swarmed,
Frogmarched us out, shocked sober, freed
From fantasy's iron cage of hate.

7

A diamond in a bed of snow,
You flash and glitter as you rage
Against your 'vile, perpetual cold',
Or else you splinter into ice,

Use words like bronchiectasis
Then run into a storm outside,
Place hailstones on my open palm
And try to force my fingers round.

8

Plath's taking her life has always upset,
If only because waste had the last word.
Nobody saw that the black-poem-a-day,
That 'Daddy', a 'statue with one grey toe',

Was a cry from the heart for some warmth
To lighten the damp clinging ashes of self,
So in the end to be beautifully plumed,
Rise red and gold like the phoenix and sing.

Runaways (2)

We blamed our failed nomadic life
In service to our art in Greece
On lack of funds to buy the peace

Even a one-star hotel might
Include, on vague abstractions such
As rule by Turks turning 'the Womb

Of Civilisation' into
A dump not worthy of the muse,
On anything short of the truth

Tabooed as too close to the bone:
Your bronchiectasis, or more
Concretely still, your chronic cold,

As everlasting as your talk
About whether to tie your tubes,
My need to be alone to write,

Your mother left in Hobart Town
With arthritis. Therefore we fled
'The Capsised Cradle of the West',

Betrayed my first love, Athens, for
Your more sophisticated Rome,
Secretly hoping that the Pope

Might work a miracle with lungs,
Decisions on fallopians,
My selfish ways, her ruined bones.

But stuck with who we are, we fought,
Nothing resolved till flying back
I heard above jet's roar Zeus storm,

'My lightning now guiding you home
Next time you run instead of face
And solve problems will strike you down!'

Release

1

Two jewels in a cage, the birds
Swung rainbow-coloured, lighting up
The dense green foliage round about,
Fluttering to the floor to preen, strut
As king and queen, to bill and coo,

Nuzzling, sleeking each other's head
And plumage, shining all the more
In splendour as po-faced we watched
Awkwardly side by side and shared
The darkness of our loveless lives.

2

I beat on the bars of wedlock
Until you released the stiff catch
And left the door open in case
The search for my 'home' proved a flop,

The first sudden plunge to the sea
Sufficient to cancel the flight.
Bright feathers still warm from your love,
Grey death is the nest I will find.

3

I waved you off to Hobart Town
And in the streets of Athens found
Spring Carnival was in the air,
With masks of heroes from the myths

Adorning budding trees, that they
Might also be renewed. I leant
Against the one I needed then,
The much-enduring Heracles,

And looked into the strengthening sun,
Felt hopeful as I closed my eyes,
Relaxed the tight lines on my face
And took my first deep breath in years.

6

An Expatriate's Lament

1

I felt like driftwood, anchorless,
Without your respiratory ills
Profoundly structuring our lives,
My keeping you in Tic-Tacs to

Mask halitosis caused by phlegm,
Your 'I'm bronchiecstatic' joke
When during sex, not taking care,
I'd cause you to fear losing yet

More breath, a seizure imminent.
And this light-headedness and lack
Of focus despite my release
From guilt and shame when bits of lung

The surgeon had to leave collapsed
And I would think best wait for death
That way instead of pillow pressed,
Temptingly easy in your case.

2

No child to show the world that we
Made love, it wasn't that, but your
Poor health from having just one lung
That drove me to abscond to Greece,

Where I, lonely in hotel rooms
Labouring to give birth to poems found
That they like you on walks with me
Almost at once ran out of breath.

3

Just once more to watch with you
Sun playing round the white boats moored
In the calm and dreaming sea,

Just once more to have you here,
My smile dancing in your eyes,
Just once more asked all the time.

4

My letter saying, 'You're too ill
To be my muse, and thus were left
Like Ariadne, that I might,
The monster slain, identify
With Theseus more deeply,' drew,

'Diseased, I much prefer the sick
To live with till the day I die,
My mother's bent, arthritic bones
At home with my displaced insides.
In you, my subtly evil spouse

Cheered by the sight of others' woes,
I found the deadliest of foes,
Your rude good health unbearable
And worthy of my wicked cold
To undermine and drive away.'

5

Worst was my paranoid outburst
Caused by your seeing more of Madge
G. Ripper, Hobart Town's bitch-bard:
'Beware of the chameleon-

Destroyer while I'm on furlough
From lung disease in ancient Greece.
As Sappho she'll break your resolve
To play Penelope to my

Odysseus, as fungus, worm,
Fly, death-watch beetle, moth wipe out
The island's leafage to make sure
No other poet can be crowned.'

6

'Please write of illnesses and deaths
Involving you on my behalf
While I'm in Hellas hunting poems,
Unless I'm first to go, as I,

Unstable, of no fixed abode,
Or character, in old age search
Through ancient myths for who I am,
And dangerously, without heed,

Identify with Daedalus,
Achilles, Hector, Theseus,
Circe, Pentheus and Orpheus,
As Agamemnon take a bath.'

7

I wished to hear dramatic news,
To have my mindscape altered by
The deaths of those I'm jealous of,
By editors accepting poems,

But very little will have changed,
Except the garden now it's cold,
Your illness only for the worse,
Unless your silence is the grave's.

8

I rang from overseas and saw
Our handset bedroom telephone
Unlifted from its cradle, pushed
Beyond your reach as laughingly
You made the beast with someone else.

Vibrantly, on and on it shrilled
Despite my calling on the dot
Of our carefully prearranged time.
I hung up and it followed me,
But now as an implacably

Silent object in my mind's eye,
As still as stone and white as bone
With rigor-mortis grin from ear
To ear, till I imagined you
Lying as dead as it in bed.

9

Crowd-watcher in cafés, I'd see
You chairs and tables distant, not
Huge seas and continents away.
Small gestures as girls nursed their drinks

Were nothing, and yet everything
I had to go on in my make-
Believe that you would change your mind
And suddenly arrive in Greece

As a surprise. The day they took
The awnings down, and those I watched
Sun glasses off, the game was up,
Since none were close to having your

Laughing-blue, light summery eyes,
But all were shades of autumn-brown,
Deciding me to keep mine on,
As dark as winter in advance.

10

White roses growing at my door
I gave to Greeks whose eyes revealed
They were received less joyfully

Than yours once showed. Discomfited,
As mere acquaintances asked to
Receive a gift, they stammered thanks,

And as I turned to go I felt
Relieved I'd left the red ones to
Die gracefully upon the stem.

11

You flew to Athens to see me,
Endured twenty hours in the air
Unable to properly breathe,

Your heart grown tired, heavier from
Not just enlarging in space left
By surgery, but from our trial

Year apart you said, after we'd
Pecked nervously and mine had sunk,
Your cough going off in my ear

Like gun shots and your head-to-toe
Black outfit registering, as did
My shadow on a wall along-

Side yours, as stooped as question marks
Deciding whether to embrace
And both stopping well short of that.

12

Mask quivering, teeth clenched to stop
Me baring them, from snarling in
Our small shared workroom such things as

'Like living with a dog inside'
When you'd bark up infected green,
Breaking my concentration to

The point of losing a good line,
But you'd twig, snap 'excuse me please,
I need to breathe.' And your *remarque*

D'escalier as you at last
Stormed out forever has remained
Memorably painful decades on:

'Don't ever dedicate a poem
To me again, since I would read
Thinking of it as poisoned bait.'

13

Our 'deathless', 'indefinable',
'Ideal' love turned to touch and talk,
Instead of being pitched beyond
Their circumscribing, harmful reach

For soul to yearn intensely for,
As once it was when our eyes shone,
Enchanted by the morning star,
All things disintegrate and rot.

14

An oleander flower fell
Onto the heart-side of my shirt
Just as I wondered if you'd write.
It should have been the bitter leaf,

The curving green blade famous for
Its poison with the power to kill,
Since silence knifing rusts with age
And festers all I think and feel.

15

When letters from your lawyers come
I philosophically agree
You need to break your promises
Too heartfelt to endure for long,

Dead-calm and abstract understand,
World-wearily forgive, include
A short poem as the final word:
'Your marriage, health, art, teaching gone,

No children to divert bleak moods,
Of course our joint-owned house is yours
In which to wear your sadness well,'
And condescendingly sign all.

7

Dashed Prospects in Crete

(For Iocasta)

A hot-as-Hades summer day,
I thought you'd buttoned to the neck
In playful, deft allusion to

Your mythical namesake's grim end.
It reinforced your silence, as,
My flowers trembling in your lap,

You sat disturbed throughout our pre-
Arranged first meeting with a view
To wedlock later if we clicked.

Pulped petals near your chair not, 'He
Loves me, he loves me nots' handwork,
You rose in haste, sought Mother's no

Less shaky arm, obliging me
To rush my acrobatic, tight-
Rope, broken Greek and baldly state

My muse's need for girls as dark
As Sophoclean tragedy.
Thus caught out, clumsily I fell,

Impaled, as you, grown more composed,
Reversed the roles, swept out and flashed
A glinting minotaur-horn smile.

Theseus

1

I'd left the dark island behind,
The family-spawned beast for dead in
The maze, with Ariadne came

To Naxos. There she'd healed my wound,
My near-emasculation from
The goring received, thwarting Fate's

Hate-warped course, it seemed at the time.
When Phaedra, parading on deck,
A trophy-horn strapped to her crotch,

Exciting the stabbed gash destroyed
My love for her sister with sex,
Persuading me she should striptease

Beneath the cliffs of Sounion
For my sire, the king of Athens.
Alternating in white and black

Sailcloth it broke the pact I'd made
With him to hoist only the one
That declared me alive or dead,

Till Aegeus, half-mad from mood
Swings jumped, a great bull of a man
Brought low that I might rule instead.

2

The man who slew the minotaur,
I womanised my way to power,
Till impotent from guilt I lost
Queen Phaedra to her lust for my

Chaste son Hippolytus, accused
Later by her of rape because
She'd failed to have her way. Then he
Was dragged to death by bolting steeds

And she committed suicide.
A hobbled beast, I potter round
And never meet a female eye,
Nor bellow when my memories of

Sweet Ariadne deeply thrust
Like daggers into open wounds
And bring me to my knees to pray
For God to deal the final blow.

For Vetta

(Elizabeth Restaurant, Hania, Crete)

1

Fleet-footed, lithe of limb, the weight-
Less ghostly way you move around
The ill-lit smoke-wreathed restaurant,
Coming and going, in and out
Of sight among support posts, guests,

Is more exciting to look at,
As fruitlessly I try to catch
Your eye not just to order food
Or be inspired to write a poem,
Than Daphne etched upon a vase

Worn thin by time and use, the scene
Ethereally faint or lost,
With only clean heels and a hint
Of lyre and tree trunk to suggest
Apollo vainly in pursuit.

2

My common sense is no defence
Against your faded, trailing dress,
Your fey Piaf street-urchin act,
The way the corner of your mouth
Projects a fag, the tilt of head

I'd love to buy a beret for,
Your breathlessness and back that aches
As to and fro you run all day
Across the cobblestones and play
The tripping clown who saves the plates,

Your sad black oversized shoes I'd
Fain kneel before with ones that fit,
Your sudden smile, as tremulous
As butterflies upon the wind,
Unnetted till the very end.

3

It's Sunday and the voices rise
In chanted unison as bells
Despatch the early morning hour
With clarity into the sky.
I think of you, my butterfly,

At different stages in your flight
As music entering my soul,
That floating upwards through the scales
Begins to waver then is still
Above the steeple's glinting point.

4

I see your face in wind-torn clouds
And cat's-paw sea, on foam-laced rocks,
Obsessively, to the extent
Of having to fight panic at

The feeling that mine's turning in
To yours, and which, if confessed to
Could cause your rarely bestowed smile
To vanish into 'Go to hell!'

5

First swim for the year, I withstood,
With my brittle white limbs, the shock,
The heart-stopping jolt of the cold,
The feeling of falling to bits,

As your face, willed out of my mind,
Uncontrolled as a dream sprang back
And had me dive deeper next time,
Never knowing what I might find.

6

Although you'd splashed it cool, your face,
Screwed up against the glare as you
Recrossed the harbour stones, was like
A piece of grain-bunched icon wood,

A cinder even, sun's refuse,
So dark and small and tight it seemed.
But in the shade, sea glistening still
Was jewellery upon your skin,

And when the smile you'd hoarded ceased
To blind me, and you'd grown from ash
Into a Cretan Tree of Life,
The knot between us was undone.

7

Psychopathic Olympians
Are everywhere in stone and seem
Expressionless, indifferent to
The sun's bright gifts of sea and sky,

Reminding me of your dead look,
The smile withheld for flowers I'd picked
And given in full public view.
I'm tempted to return the same

Impeccably blank heartlessness
When next in front of guests you bless
Me with a smile of your esteem.
But when it came to it I'd fail

To find the nerve to feign the lie
And slay you with a blind cold stare,
Collapsing somewhere in between
A wobbly grin and a grimace.

8

Your actual flesh-and-blood face spoilt
By all-too-human moods is best
Encapsulated timelessly,
Beyond the reach of transience,

In durable material
With economically drawn lines,
And only ever glimpsed in art,
Now that I've failed to win your hand.

Femme Fatale

(On revisiting Zonar's Café, Athens)

1

The girl with the mulberry patch
That's half her face still sits out life
In thrall to mirrors on the walls,
Since no one else after the first

Rude stare looks back except myself,
And I with my Van Diemen's Land's
Triangular-shaped red birthmark
Evoking convicts flogged and hanged

Don't count because it doesn't show
Beneath the collar round my neck.
The only way I have to break
Her trance, to catch and hold her eye

As a disfigured soul, a mate,
Is to summon blushes of shame
Up from the roots of mine, suffuse
Her looking glass and mingle stains.

2

A vast brown varnished tomb relieved
By mirrors for loners to live
Companionably in, I sit
Reflected red-faced alongside

The girl with the mulberry patch.
In reverie for hours beneath
A broken dusty fan that's like
A fat moth's corpse, she is, despite

Being as unstirring as it
The fairest of them all. And I,
If my Hell's Gates'-singed soul had wings
And she from her cocoon of grief

Once met my longing eyes, would kiss
And wake her as though from a curse,
Change her into a butterfly
To join me fluttering in the air.

3

All day we'd share a mirror, or
A glossy, lacquered panel of
Wood in between if none were free,
And never was I first to leave,
While she played Eurydice, gone,

Or Enkidu, departed, dead
Without so much as glancing back,
And I, deserted Gilgamesh,
Or Orpheus, reflected once
More upon loss and loneliness.

4

Although life lived in mirrors kept
Us from the monstrous world outside,
One day I wondered if the beast
We like to think we know is best,

Since noting that I swallowed hard,
And that my Adam's apple shook
From unrequited love, she licked
At the reflection of it, curled

Moist mulberry-stained lips in disdain,
Vanishing, to be once again
Alone in vacant sheets of glass,
Cutting me to the very core.

5

Casting her as a femme fatale,
The gorgon Medusa, myself
As Perseus, I found her as
A reflection trying to tone

Down with a powder puff the side
Of her face marked a mottled blue.
Alerted to my threatening look,
Her gaze replied, but before she

Could turn, transform to stone, I glanced
Decapitatingly till glass
Ran red, reached in, grabbed, lifted, waved
The head aloft for all to see.

8

Rendezvous in Nice

(For Dr Ivana Gajdošová)

1

Pfizer Bayer Sandoz Roche
Lille Merck, drug corporation gods
As bloodless, abstract and remote
As merger deals, begrudge the funds

Enabling cardiologists,
For whom, beyond financial health,
They'll never have a need, to meet,
Confer, and have a nice time for

A week in Nice. Signed up, you walk
Squeegeed red rug and fuss when white
Shoes crimson, but not over me,
Who didn't think to bring you flowers,

Though we've not met for ages since
Our marriage of convenience
And tense exchange of 'heartfelt' vows.
I fail to rally with my coat,

Or arms, to blush and match footwear,
And in our unstarred hotel make,
Instead of love, jokes about botched
Transplants, and wish I'd never come.

2

(The Russian Orthodox Church of St Nicholas, Nice)

O church of tenderness and hope,
Where angels put aside their swords
And Mary from her pride of place
Upon the dome, face tensely grave,

In great anxiety of soul
Beseeches us to keep the faith
No matter how life seems to mock
Its claims, where Bach's 'Jesu Joy' wrung,

From my heart chilled to stone, the tears
Begrudged by it for years, let them
Light yet another chance to love
As candles shedding theirs the dark.

A Need to Explain

Mushrooming with you in Czech woods
I sensed your irritation when,
As a new chum, I had to ask,

Each time I plucked a different type
Of penis shape up by its roots,
If it were edible or not.

Indeed, I felt tempted to shut
Your mouth with one that had a grey,
Tripe-textured slug adhering to

Its underside. Perhaps this was,
In conjunction with looking, just
Before going to bed that night,

At Michelangelo's *Fall*, where
A serpent with a woman's head
Proffers the apple, why I lapsed

Into my childhood summer sport
In Tasmania, and dreamt I struck
And struck a black snake into bits.

Belvedere Gardens, Vienna

Though horse chestnuts are aureoled
With gold round rusting foliage,
Black, column-straight trunks make them shrines

To night as ravens and I stand
Beneath a chilling cobalt sky.
Bells peal, and garden sphinxes ask,

'Why can't the lion and lamb lie down
In harmony again?' Despite
My terse 'because they never did',

The question stays. And I too now
We've quarrelled and you've gone to Prague.
Your hair imagined as these tree

Leaves falling, swept by death-thin men
Into brown heaps, blackbirds alight
And hop about on cold bare limbs

In ownership, as news sinks in
That you have cancer and your course
In chemotherapy's begun.

For my Czech Stepdaughter

1

The snow corkscrewing down to melt
On contact with earth's mushy corpse,
Like suiciding worms, evokes
Memories of unsuccessful sex

In old age with mother-wife, whose
Bad breath and colonostomy
Have rubbed my nose for too long in
The cancer of reality.

I need to see you as the trees,
That leafless mean you've shed your tears,
Their young roots bared that you will run
Away with me when she is dead.

2

I have always loved the blackbird,
If not as such, then surely for
Symbolising death beautifully,
And now you're turning into them,

Tall thin dark, anorexic girl,
As elegantly angular
And stooping slightly as the one
I watch searching the snow for food

And flying off alone still starved.
This afternoon, as usual on
My solitary walk, I'll hope,
In an otherwise empty park,

To meet you hopping nervously.
I've only old man's crumbs, but you
Are welcome if you'll help me die
As I have lived, in love with night.

3

On Christmas Eve, the glasses filled,
Carp served, and 'Spiritual Song'
By James McAuley well in mind –

'Reunited friends partake
In the fresh blue trout and wine,
Green-golden wine,

Of endless love, its meal and sign' –
My knife and fork, to make room, were
Edged off the table to my lap.

Though different fish, poem's meaning matched
Your visit after months away,
My dark soul's brightening as you picked

The latter up and put it back,
But left, as our eyes met and shared
A moment's knowing, then flashed 'No!',

The first lodged upright, all to me,
So terrible to mother-wife
Would be the wound of outraged trust.

4

I'm ill, with money in my will
For you. Meanwhile, a blackbird, your
Familiar perches on the bed-
Room windowsill, but whether its

Naturally mistrustful, shy,
Forgivably greedy regard
Contains a trace of true concern
Is difficult to tell. Then through

A dulled glass separating door
I watch as you prepare my meal
For mother-wife, though never you,
To bring in with cruel-knowing smile,

Despite it being just my mind
Your movements these days stir beyond
The power of decency to quell.
Your face unread still as it turns

Towards me like the moon in cloud,
I check your sign, find two and feel
I've flown in to be alone
With you to look you in the eye.

In Memory of Dr Ivana Gajdošová 1944–2013

1

My wife's terminal cancer meant
In our small flat she seemed to be
Forever in the lavatory.
I didn't chicken out, but stayed

To comfort, shop, cook, wash-up, clean
And look on helplessly, a prey
To thoughts so shaming, deeply black,
So disillusioning, I did

My best to bury them with her.
Yet three years on, persisting still,
Denying me the heights from which
I used to idealise her as

A Madonna-like, golden-haired
Cardiologist caring for
Patients as Mary did for Christ,
Heart-felt they overwhelm me with

'All is of equal worthlessness,'
As when Swift, maddened by despair
Cut short a poem praising his pure
Love with 'but Celia, Celia shits.'

2

I walk as usual, now you've gone,
Leaf in hand, on slippery rocks
Around the bay, the siren-waves
Whispering as huskily as your
Broken Czech-English that I loved,

'Why not rejoin me, stranded as
You are again in loneliness
I saved you from for twenty years?'
Afraid, I brush you off, crushed to
Bits by my tightly clenched damp palm,

And watch you blown into a sky
Dark as my mood, or float away,
Voice changing to an angry deep
Reproachful note I also knew:
'A poor reward for what I did!'

3

Uneasy on a gloomy bush-
Bound track I relived childhood fears
Of cannibal Gabbett escaped
From Hell's Gates in Marcus Clarke's *For
The Term of His Natural Life*,

Who running out of mates' meat might
Wolf down the butterflies I loved,
When one lit golden as a patch
Of sunlight on my outstretched hand:
You, come back in this form to save!

That night I dreamt of you enthroned
On high before descending in
Haloed glory, the soles of your
Tensely arched feet walking on air
As white as Christ's uplifted from

The sea to reach Peter in need,
As in a Sunday school image
Or painting by Tiepolo.
Then on the point of vanishing,
Showing the cleanest pair of heels

To the communist world you loathed,
Turning you saw me waiting in
Your packed reception room and crooked
Your doctor's finger, summoning,
And I woke feeling purged of grief.

9

A Thank You to a Polish Musician

Hesitantly I agree
To something I've not done before:
Fill in by fingering a screen
Answers to questions on how folk

Rate visiting Hobart's museum.
Sensitively, patiently
You teach the way to gently touch
The iPod until I alone

Can quickly get it to respond.
As thanks for help with your research
You email when and where Bach next
With Mendelssohn are to be heard.

Depressed still one year after my
Czech wife's demise, I will myself
To make the effort, and, surprise,
You're first violinist, and I watch

As much as listen as you play,
Brought back to life because you share
In her Slavonic, pure high-brow,
Centuries-long developed taste

In music, and with whom I went
To such concerts for two decades.
And now, with you accompanying
The rhythm of these lines, here in

Return's a song for you and her:
An extraordinary sky
Of golden-blue set in the depths,
The heart of winter like a jewel,

Heralds spring with trumpets, and lights,
As did Christ's Passion in the church
Where you so elegantly bowed,
With hope, while twigs at ends of bare

Upthrusting branches in the park
My flat looks on stretch forth to warmth,
And buds exposed blush pink with pride
As more and more I venture out.

Breaking the Ice
(For HGF)

A tory and a monarchist,
But also an ex-rival for
Your troth, I sat next to you at

The launch of the successful one's
Book on breaking the ice as first
Australian ambassador to

China during the Whitlam years.
And not once did we dare to steal
A glance and share a moment, so

Brittle and cold the atmosphere
We might have snapped, the temperature
Dropping as the event went on,

And all compounded by our just
Having accidentally met
A good half-century since I

Had passed out at your wedding drunk
From disappointment, and your dad
Half-dragging, escorted me down

My old school's chapel aisle, a thaw
Possible only when we rose
As stiff as icicles to clap,

Managing somehow, limbs intact,
To peck, shake hands, shuffle away,
I with the shadow of the right.

For Robyn Mathison

Poemless for months, today your out-
Of-turn surprise postcard flown in
From the wintry blue gave me one
Featuring a robin redbreast.

I perched it shy and spry as your
Familiar on my unused desk,
Watching its head that seemed to cock
This way and that, expressing doubt

As to whether I'd heard the note
It deftly sounded, pure and sure
As your muse's, to tune me for
This long overdue song of thanks.

Aesthetically Speaking

With her Uluru Rock-red hair,
A hard-as-nails, tigerish, done-
It-tough, grudging-mean bitter look,
The politician wearing T

V warpaint's a sickly take on
Australia's Aborigines,
Their racist foe with snarling clown's
Carrot-hued wig and chalky white

Death-face caricaturing them.
And corroboree mask removed,
As news of the behaviour of
Her low-life followers comes in,

Collapsing, she's the ugliness
In outback women, gutted, stripped
Of Drysdale's, Lawson's tributes to
Drovers' wives, grit, compassion mocked

By this slattern deserving of
A black or jihadist behind
A drought-honed tree ready to spear
Or blow to bits her water tank,

As gazing blotto she blurs more
A heat-hazed land, the kids and dogs
Knowing not to raise dust near her,
Waiting, white-trash, food cheap booze,

In a loud floral frock, one of
Her brute-bloke's sheep-faced sorry-gifts,
For him to come, weeks or months late,
Reeking of dags sweat grog whores to

Hungover pulp her lizard-lipped
Chainsaw-whining nagging mouth quiet,
Easily the most provocative,
Distasteful part of this shrew's kit.

Adam Tempted to Give Eve Flowers

I must be careful not to thank
Her too effusively, with say
The presentation of a bunch
Of even thornless roses for

Just phoning to ask how I am,
Which, lonely, I was wanting to
See as a sexual overture.
Since females have decided that

Men causing them to blush and sigh,
To suffer agonies of joy,
Have embarrassed, harassed, and should
Be charged accordingly forthwith.

St Helen's Road

(For fair sweet Molly Brown)

My walk's a hobble, all pass save
Molly who slows to greet and chat
And leaves me wondering if I should,

Next time we meet by chance, give way-
Side flowers in a bid to seduce,
Or act my age and see her as

A fresh-faced angel stepped out of
A quattrocento master's work,
As even sent by higher powers

To enliven what often seems
A lonely road that only can
End in the cul-de-sac of death.

www.ingramcontent.com/pod-product-compliance
Lightning Source LLC
Chambersburg PA
CBHW070919080526
44589CB00013B/1370